THE UNOFFICIAL SCRIVENER WORKBOOK

by
Michael J. Carlson

Copyright

ISBN-10: 1530582725
ISBN-13: 978-1530582723

Printed in the United States of America
Book design by Michael Jervis
Cover art courtesy of: literatureandlatte.com

Disclaimer/Limit of Liability:

THE UNOFFICIAL SCRIVENER WORKBOOK

DEDICATION

To Sparkle, without whose patience and encouragement, none of this would be possible.

A special thanks to the people at Scrivener who have granted me permission to use their name and an altered version of their logo on the cover and in this book.

Contents

SECTION 1

SECTION 2

SECTION 3

SECTION 4

SECTION 1

Philosophy

To quote from the Scrivener Manual:

> "Most word processors and text editors aimed at writers assume the creative process will take place in linear form; that is, they assume that the writer knows how his or her work will begin and will start at the beginning and continue through until reaching the end, and for those that do work that way, they assume that a linear form is a useful format for a text that spans hundreds of pages. Planning and restructuring is therefore forced into a separate workflow—the writer must either plan before beginning and keep track of hundreds of different files using the computer or face the laborious task of cutting and pasting numerous chunks of text to restructure a long piece of work at the end. For shorter pieces of writing, this is not a massive problem, but for longer texts—such as novels or academic theses—the writer can often find him- or herself battling against the tools of their trade. What a word processor does get right is in not presuming anything of your working methods. It is, at the core, ruthlessly simple.
>
> Scrivener is part of a new breed of writing software which focusses more on providing a solid open-ended writing tool (as the word processor does) rather than a writing process, which presumes a system upon you. As with a word processor, there are no chapters or sections

or scenes; how you use the software determines these things, not some feature baked into the program. Scrivener's design is fairly unique in that it easily provides a platform for writers of many philosophies and disciplines. It's a tool that works equally well for a doctoral dissertation, as it does for writing a short story or a screenplay."

Most people, who set out to write a novel do so in either Microsoft Word or one of the free, open source variants, like Open Office, or Libre Office. Most people also find out pretty quickly that using a word processor is, shall we say, a less than ideal tool for writing a novel-length work. To paraphrase Mick "Crocodile" Dundee, "You can do it, but it always gives me gas."

I mean, just take saving your work. There are only two ways you can save a novel-length work with a word processor; either as one really long file or as a bunch of text files in a folder. I mean, really. If you move a scene in the former, you run the risk of accidentally copying something else before you paste it where you wanted it and losing the scene completely. Or if you forget to cut it from the first place, you could end up with two identical scenes, or something equally ridiculous.

Not to mention, what do you do with your research, your descriptions of characters' physical attributes, etc? Or maybe you're one of those who likes to look around on the Web for a picture that looks like how you envision your character. Where do you put that, in the same folder as the other stuff? How about web pages or search results? What about that PDF or all the information about the French national train system? Where's that going? Stuff gets misplaced, browser bookmarks fill up, and we cross our fingers every time we decide to change our main character's eye color that they won't go from blue eyes to green and back again.

Until recently, there wasn't much choice. The word processor (any word processor) was an imperfect tool, but any of them were light years ahead of you father's Smith-Corona electric (oh, wait. I had a Smith-Corona electric typewriter). The big improvement going from the electric typewriter to the word processor was the ability to correct typos and misspelled words without resorting to white paint and an itty bitty brush. And we could actually move a block of text to a different place not involving either scissors or a boat-load of re-typing.

Seemed like a miracle at the time. Damn. But we knew there had to be a better way, and darned if a couple of guys from the UK didn't come up with it (clever monkeys, those Brits). So, Scrivener was born.

Scrivener was originally designed for the Mac, which torqued off a bunch of people who had invested in Microsoft products. So, we now have a version for each. And, I'm pretty sure, those same clever Brits realized the Windows people would be willing to trade body parts for a novel organizing program which worked.

I'm told they're similar enough you can go from one to the other without getting lost. I haven't used the Windows version. For my part, the Redmond Behemoth and I parted ways over a decade ago, and I never looked back. Be that as it may, Scrivener gives the writing community a tool for organizing something as big as a novel, including the text, research, photos, web pages, sound bites, and even movies.

Holy crap.

The program is so versatile, it can be customized to work almost any way the individual can. And, at the time of this writing, still comes in at $45 for the Mac version, $40 for the windows counterpart, and an iOS version for $20. There's even a free beta version for the Linux wing nuts out there (we know who we are).

Sure, there are other novel organizing software programs, and most of them work pretty well, but none I've tried (and I've tried a lot of writing software) comes close to Scrivener in terms of robustness and versatility.

THE UNOFFICIAL SCRIVENER WORKBOOK

If you're reading this, you either bought Scrivener (three cheers and a tiger for you) or you're considering it. Go on, dude download it. There's a 30-day trial. What have you got to lose, but an inefficient way of doing things? Yeah, it's scary at first, especially the first time, but so was sex, and that turned out okay for the most part.

Besides, what if it does everything everybody say it does? Wouldn't *that* be cool?

MICHAEL J. CARLSON

Why this Workbook?

This workbook is set up similarly to a college laboratory workbook. The text and most of the illustrations are based on The Scrivener Manual and The Interactive Tutorial included with your version of Scrivener. This book is structured as a series of exercises that will, hopefully, lead you to a solid, basic, understanding of how to use Scrivener on a daily basis. In the process, you'll learn how to set up your own novel template to use as you wish, and change at any time to suit your needs.

This workbook is an UNOFFICIAL version. That means, the opinions, bad jokes, dumb errors (both the typos and errors in judgment), and rants against Microsoft Word are all on me. The good people who brought you Scrivener had nothing to do with the creation of this workbook or my odd sense of humor. Having said that, this workbook refers extensively, if indirectly, to the Scrivener Manual and the Interactive Tutorial. Most of what I cover here is contained there without the pretty pictures. Also, this workbook only scratches the surface of what Scrivener is capable of. I've been using it almost every day for six years in two versions, and I still regularly learn new things it'll do.

Please refer to the Scrivener manual or the interactive tutorial for issues not addressed in this workbook. The Scrivener website: litteratureandlatte.com, has links to various YouTube videos which cover the concepts here (the section on setting up Compile is almost a transcript of the YouTube video). The forums are also a good place to go looking for the answers to life's questions. If all else fails, the good folks who brought you Scrivener have a contact link. For questions regarding this text, I can be reached at michael@mjcarlson.com.

I've found the Scrivener community to be friendly and helpful toward newbies with questions. Everything I've presented in this workbook is something I had to learn, often more than once. Don't be ashamed to ask questions. In this case, the converse of the old adage is true: "It's better to ask a question and be thought a fool, than to remain quiet and remove all doubt."

Happy Trails.

Extra space. Be creative:

MICHAEL J. CARLSON

Mac vs Windows

Anyone who's used both Operating Systems will notice similarities and differences in the underlying philosophies. Scrivener was originally written for Mac, with the Windows version coming later (there's also a beta version for Linux). This Workbook was written on a Mac, so some of the references will be different if you're using the Windows version. I've made every effort to cover both where there are major differences. If I missed anything, apologies.

At the time of this writing, the most current versions of Scrivener are:

Mac: version 1.5.4
Mac OS X 10.4-10.6 PPC machines (License no longer available for purchase)

Mac: version 2.5
Mac OS X 10.4-10.5 PPC machines (License still available through literatureandlatte.com)

Mac: version 2.7.0
Mac OS X 10.6 and later

Windows: version 1.9
Windows XP, Vista, 7, 8, 8.1, and Windows 10

Linux: version 1.9.0.1 BETA
Linux Debian and Ubuntu variations

iOS
Scrivener for iOS was released within the past month prior to the final editing of this book. While I have no direct knowledge of how the application works, I'm confident that if literature & latte put it out, it works.

Keyboard shortcuts

While not necessary to use Scrivener, keyboard shortcuts are designed to save time, and will occasionally be referred to in the Workbook. I'll try to keep their use to a minimum, but you may want to familiarize yourself with some of the basics, like: CMD+Z (pressing the COMMAND key and the Z key simultaneously). This causes Scrivener (and most word processors) to undo the most recent action, much like mouse-clicking the little left-pointing arrow. Besides, if you memorize a couple of keyboard shortcuts, you'll look really cool to your non-geek friends. Way worth it.

Please note: On machines using Microsoft Windows, the COMMAND (CMD) key becomes the CONTROL (CTRL) key, so CMD+Z becomes CTRL+Z on those computers. I've included some very basic, simple shortcuts. These are:

CMD+A (CTRL+A) = Select all
CMD+B (CTRL+B) = Make selected text bold
CMD+C (CTRL+C) = Copy selected text
CMD+I (CTRL+I) = Make selected text italic
CMD+K (CTRL+K) = Split at selection
CMD+N (CTRL+N) = Create a new text file
CMD+S (CTRL+S) = Save the thing you're working on
CMD+U (CTRL+U) = Underline selected text
CMD+V (CTRL+V) = Paste selected text
CMD+X (CTRL+X) = Cut selected text
CMD+Z (CTRL+Z) = Undo most recent action
CMD+1 (CTRL+1) = Open Scrivenings view (Editor screen)
CMD+2 (CTRL+2) = Open Corkboard view
CMD+3 (CTRL+3) = Open Outliner view

Oh, one really cool one if you have a Mac:
CMD+M = minimizes the window you're working in. I don't think there's a similar shortcut in Windows, so :P

Terms and Conventions

Most of this section is taken verbatim from the Scrivener Manual. The version this workbook was created on was 2.3 for Mac. If you have the Windows version, you'll likely have a lower number version number unless this project has very much outlived me. I'm not sure how I'd feel about that, but I won't be around for comment, in any event. Oh, I also took the liberty of correcting those misspelled-by-the-British words, like "customise."

Whenever the documentation refers to an action which must be taken by you, the visible name for the action are formatted like so: Project > Show Project Targets. Button labels, menu items, and keyboard shortcuts are displayed in this fashion.

Menus are displayed in a hierarchy using the " > " character to separate top-level, sub-menu, and items. Example: To convert a range of selected text to uppercase, invoke the Format > Convert > To Uppercase command. And they'll be in this pretty blue color (but only in the ebook version).

Keyboard shortcuts will use the following symbols:

CMD+ (Mac) or CTRL+ (Windows)

The Command key, or the Apple key, is located directly to the left and right of your spacebar. Its symbol looks like a 4-leaf clover sort of if you squint.

The Option key is also labeled the Alt key on some keyboards, depending on which country you purchased your Mac from. Some laptops only have one Option key on the left side.

Control is usually located to the left and right of the Option keys on their respective side. Some laptops only have one Control key between the Option key and the Fn key on the left side.

The Shift keys are rarely used by themselves in shortcuts but are often used in combination with other modifier keys.

When a keyboard shortcut requires a modifier key (most do), they will be printed together. Example: CMD+A means you should hold down the modifier key (the Command key) and then tap the A key on your keyboard. The "+" is only there to indicate both keys are pressed together. If you're using a machine running Windows, merely substitute CTRL (the Control key) for CMD.

Interface elements will be capitalized as proper nouns to help differentiate them from standard nouns when appropriate. A Collection is an interface element, while the word "collection" is used to indicate a casual grouping of items, like text files, politicians, or monkeys, and not a formal Collection.

Some of the names for various elements within Scrivener are customizable on a per project basis, and how you name these will impact much of the interface. A good example is the Draft, AKA the place where your manuscript in progress is built. This can be called whatever you like, and what you name it will impact the names of menu items referring to it. In all cases, this documentation will refer to these malleable elements by their default names.

And yes, there will be monkeys.

The Fiction Novel

Most of you will be writing fiction novels, which Scrivener is perfectly suited for. Please note, there are several perfectly functional fiction templates already available in Scrivener, which can be used as is, or modified and saved as your very own template. Several other templates are available from individuals on the Internet. I shouldn't have to warn you about accepting code from strangers, any more than I should have to warn you about accepting rides from strange men in vans, wearing trench coats and sunglasses, who offer you candy. Did someone say candy?

Anyway, caveat emptor, or let the downloader beware, or something like that. Just be careful. Now, if you'll excuse me, there's a guy in a black van, with a bag of Skittles, at the curb. Be right back.

Short Fiction

You don't hear much about Scrivener being used for short fiction (short stories and novellas), but there's no reason you can't. All that stuff about long fiction applies here, too. Hey, anybody know anyone who wants to buy a used black van? It just needs the interior cleaned and maybe a few skittles vacuumed up. The former owner went away to another country—France, or Canada, I think, but he wanted me to get rid of his van. He kept his knife.

Non-fiction

Is mostly boring, but necessary, kind of like kissing your mother on her birthday. But Scrivener does a great job with a PhD thesis or a simple how-to workbook and everything in between. Scrivener's organizing tools are well-suited to structuring non-fiction works.

Screenplays

While we also don't hear much about Scrivener in terms of writing screenplays, it's fully capable of exporting to Final Draft (the industry standard).

SECTION 2

Getting familiar with Scrivener

In this first section, we'll just be looking around at various Scrivener functions and becoming comfortable with the very basics. I made the illustrations on a Macbook Pro using Scrivener 2.3. Your Windows version will look slightly different.

We'll assume you've installed Scrivener to your machine, 'cause otherwise, why are you even reading this? Okay, take a deep breath. In this section, we're going to get comfortable with the interface. Open scrivener. You'll see something like Figure 1:

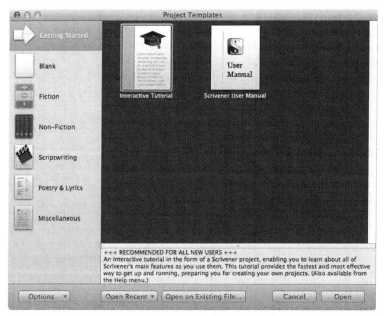

Figure 1: The Template Wizard

You'll notice a light blue column on the left. This column contains different templates you may want for various projects, for instance:

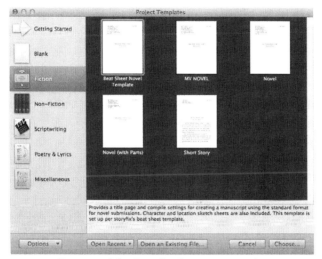

Figure 2: The Standard Fiction templates

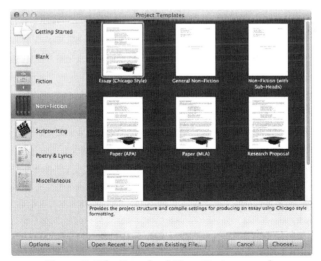

Figure 3: The Standard Non-Fiction templates

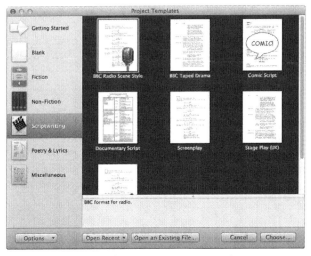

Figure 4: The Scriptwriting templates

And the one we'll be using:

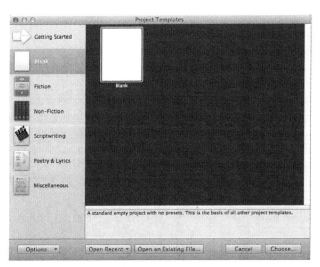

Figure 5: The Blank Template Wizard

We'll use the Blank template, as we'll be setting up our own version of a novel template. The importance of having your very own template will become apparent. Keep in mind, though, this template, as well as the others, can be changed according to your needs, and you can save these changed templates as your very own as you go. Remember, Scrivener is built to work for you, not the other way around.

Keep this one fact in mind: Scrivener is not Microsoft Word. Nor is it just a simple (or bloated) word processor. It's a novel organizing as well as novel writing software, and about three other software programs you'd expect to pay money for if you bought them individually. If you try to set up Scrivener like you did MS Word (or Open Office, Libre Office, et al) you will only succeed in pissing yourself off and wasting time. The single most important thing you can remember when setting Scrivener up is this:

Composition (the act of producing a work of text) and typesetting (arranging and formatting type to be printed) are two distinct conceptual entities which the modern word processor has conflated into one process. This is important enough to bear mentioning again:

Composition and **Typesetting** are two distinct conceptual entities which your word processor has conflated into one process. Scrivener re-separates those two processes.

What does that mean? Composition is the writing part of writing where you sit your backside in a chair and put words on a screen. Composition is not about font, or size, or format or any of that. It's about the words, story, and characters. Typesetting is about what the letters look like on the page. It used to be done in the back rooms of presses by gnarled old men in long leather aprons, using molten lead and machines the size of semi-trailers. Until word processors came along, and then your grandmother got to fiddle around with pretty fonts and went all "Ooo, look at the colors. I'll bet this pink is really pretty with this Papyrus 16-point." Arrrgh.

Anyway…

The formatting in the Editor window you'll be looking at is just and only for you. Set it up any way you like. What the text formatting in the Editor screen looks like has no bearing whatsoever on what the compiler will do to your text at the end. The two things are separate processes, controlled in different parts of the program. Keep one thing in mind though. If you get to the end and use copy/paste to get your manuscript out of Scrivener and, into MS Word, Open Office, or any of the eighty or so word processors on the market, your Editor formatting will go along, including the 16-point Helvetica font that will make your editor cringe and mutter embarrassing expletives.

So, let's get going. Double-click the Blank icon. You should get something like Figure 6:

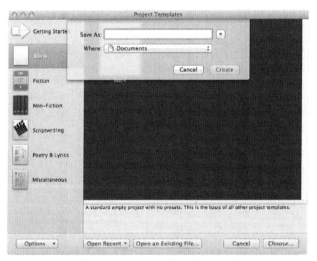

Figure 6: Name Your Project

You'll have to name your project before we get started. Things in Scrivener are projects, not documents, remember? So, because this will be your novel template, let's give it an imaginative, writerly name, like My Novel Template, or "_Insert Your Name Here_" Novel Template. I suppose you could name it Bibbly-Bobbly, but, *really*? Click Create. Now…

The Main Window

Once you've created and named your new project, you'll see something like Figure 7:

Figure 7: The Main Interface

You'll notice some things may seem familiar from your old word processor days, like the Toolbar (1), Format bar (2), and Editor screen (3). You'll also see some new things, unique to Scrivener, like the Binder (4), and Inspector (5).

Quickly; we'll spend the next few sections looking at these parts of the interface and familiarizing ourselves with them. While the may look similar to what you've seen in the past, there are some significant differences. If you're comfortable with Scrivener's interface, you may want to skip over this section and jump right to getting started.

Let's examine each of these things individually and discover what they do.

The Toolbar

Figure 8: The Toolbar

The Toolbar should look familiar to anyone who's used a word processor (I'm guessing pretty much, everybody at this point). But, Scrivener's is a bit different, and surprise (if you're used to MS Word), the things available in the Toolbar are all designed to be helpful—to you. If you right-click the Toolbar (or, alternatively click View > Customize Toolbar at the bottom), you'll see the Customize Toolbar popup window. There's a bunch of other, useful writing aids available here. I'll refer you to the Scrivener Manual for an explanation of what each is and what they all do. That's beyond the scope of this workbook.

Adding too many icons can make the Toolbar too busy, so only add what you think you'll need. This is the Toolbar I use. From left to right, these are:

The Binder. You use this button to make the Binder visible/invisible. I personally like it sitting there, reminding me where I am, but that's me. The next button is Collections. Don't worry about that one for now. The same is true of Layouts. I find Add very useful. This is how you add chapters and scenes to the Binder. To add a chapter, you'll click and hold, dragging the cursor over the "folder" icon. To add a scene, you just click the green button.

The Trash button is pretty self-explanatory. You select some offending scene or drivel in the Binder, click the Trash button, and text is eradicated (not really. It's in the trash folder at the bottom of the Binder). It'll stay right there until you empty the trash, but once it's gone, it's gone.

Compose is so cool, it gets its own section, later in the workbook.

The Keywords button does what you'd expect. I don't use it much, mostly because the Keywords button puts the search results where the Binder normally sits, and I use the Binder a lot.

Quick Reference gives you a pop-up window of what you're working on, which seems like a waste of a good button. But consider—what if you're working on one scene and think you need to make a change to another one? Or, you want a floating window with your main character's photo in it. You have both open.

Comment is another uber-cool button. We'll get to it soon.

Wrap is helpful for longer titles in your synopsis, corkboard, or outlining mode. Wrap will also make your text look more like a word processor, but I don't find this function very helpful. We'll get to the others later when we talk about organizing.

Compile is for the end. Be patient, Grasshopper.

Dictionary is also just what you'd think. You select a word, click Dictionary, and you get the definition or thesaurus in a popup window.

Toggle Ruler puts the little ruler at the top of the editor, so you know where your indents are, etc.

Fonts. Again, just what you'd expect.

View Mode is probably the most powerful thing on the Toolbar, and what makes Scrivener more than a word processor. It also gets its own section where we'll be extensively playing with this one.

Further off to the right (for you wide-screen people) is a Search box and the Inspector button. The Inspector hides/shows the Inspector column. Before you hide it and forget it, as I did for a year and a half, remember, the Inspector and Binder columns are what makes Scrivener more powerful than a simple word processor. You'll be amazed at what it can do. Really.

This ends our tour of the Toolbar. Now we move onto the Format bar.

The Format Bar

Figure 9: The Format Bar

The Format bar is probably the thing (other than the editor box) most familiar to people who use a word processor. It's also the most misunderstood, and probably the most improperly used thing people who routinely use a word processor use. It's responsible for most of the error messages when uploading an eBook for conversion. We're going to spend a few boring minutes finding out what the Format bar is actually good for. Unless you're familiar with setting Styles in your current word processor, you're making a mistake every time you use this thing. This is according to all three independent editors I've worked with and The Smashwords Style Guide, by Mark Coker. So, let's get into it and make it work for us.

Historical perspective

Back when the Earth was still a cooling molten ball of magma, word processors usurped the position enjoyed by electric typewriters. For those born after 1980, those were a combination keyboard and printer that gave output in real-time, on hard copy. Anyway, in the "good old days," one sat at a word processor and typed text into the file, as we do now. Instead of simply attaching the manuscript to an email when it was finished, we had to print the whole thing out, put it in an appropriately sized envelope, and snail-mail it to wherever it was going. As I said, the Dark Ages.

The buzzword at that time was "WYSIWYG." This is an acronym for What You See Is What You Get. WYSIWYG meant whatever appeared on your screen was exactly what your printer put onto paper. What few people know, is that ALL word processors' formatting are affected by several things outside your control, including your particular printer settings. So, your perfectly formatted and paginated manuscript you saved in .doc format (Word format to the non-geeks) is absolutely NOT what your editor will see when he/she opens your attachment. This is because those unseen settings are different on his/her computer.

There will always be small (and sometimes not so small) differences in formatting and pagination between machines and even different word processors or different versions of the same word processor. Microsoft Word is probably the worst offender, but they all do it to some degree. That's why .pdf formatting was invented—a .pdf document remains the same on every machine, no matter the settings or the operating system (however, if you open up a .pdf document on a Mac, in Preview, sometimes the under the hood formatting you can't see will do odd things to your great American Novel's formatting). Really funny to see, sometimes. Just sayin'.

How do we fix this word processor mess?

Something surprisingly simple. According to Mark Coker's Smashwords Style Guide, the easiest way for you word processor die-hards to accomplish this is to copy/paste your document into Notepad on your Windows machine (or Text Edit on a Mac). Then you re-copy/paste it back into MS Word and apply Styles. Notepad/Text Edit will strip ALL the formatting away. It's a similar concept to throwing the baby out with the bathwater, and it's called "The Nuclear Method" for good reason.

But it works. Mac users can download a copy of Bean word processor. Paste your document into Bean, and click "Remove All Styles." You'll be shocked how different your manuscript can look. Instead of pasting your text into MS Word, you could paste it directly into Scrivener from Notepad, Text Edit, or Bean if you wished, or make an .rtf version and import it into Scrivener.

Importing into Scrivener also strips most of the bad formatting away, leaving the rest relatively easy to fix. Copy/paste from MS Word into Scrivener's editor window won't accomplish this, so be forewarned. However, setting Presets in Scrivener (its version of Styles) will remove most of the icky formatting. There's a section on this a bit later.

Let's take a look at another tool just as powerful—the Binder.

The Binder

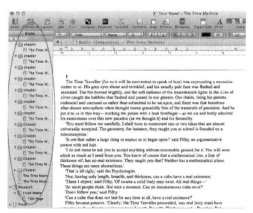

Figure 10: The Binder

The Binder is the document browser on the left of the main window where you can organize your files (by default it is colored a pale blue when the project window is active). It allows you to structure and rearrange your work. The Binder behaves like a three-ring binder in the real world. This's where you'll add folders, files, and Research. The trash is also stored in the Binder until you empty it.

It's easy to add a folder. Click and hold the green (+) sign in the toolbar until you see a window pop up containing a folder icon. Slide the mouse to that icon and a new folder will appear in the binder (New Folder). Now, add a text file to the new folder. Don't start adding your text to the folder level as it won't compile properly at the end. We'll get to that part later, trust me.

You can rename the folders and files easily by double-clicking on each. Try it now. Name the folder "Bevis" and the text file "Butthead." Don't number them. You'll understand why not in a minute. Let's add some text. Single-click the Butthead file to get to the Editor window.

The Editor

Figure 11: The Editor Window

The Editor window should be familiar to anyone who's ever used a word processor. This is where the text goes. There are three ways to get text into Scrivener. (1) by typing, (2) If you have a manuscript saved from a word processor (dare I say Microsoft Word?) you can drag and drop text into either the file in the Binder or onto the Editor window and it will import. There's a third way: click File > Import > Files. Find your manuscript and Scrivener will import it to your folder.

The Inspector

Figure 12: The Inspector

The Inspector is the area on the far right. If yours is invisible, Click the blue button which says, oddly enough, "Inspector."

If you look closely, you'll notice the uppermost line at the top of the column says "Synopsis." This is one of the Inspector's main functions; it works in connection with the Corkboard and Outliner view to assist you in writing and organizing your scenes.

You can do a lot of cool things using this area of Scrivener, but for now, we'll focus on its organizing capabilities. Click on the topmost line. In here, you can write the scene name, i.e. Vader captures Leia. I'd strongly recommend you enter information pertaining to YOUR book and not that one, unless possibly you're Kevin J. Anderson. Otherwise, the Lucas people will find you and it won't be pretty.

Go ahead, type something in there. I like to use the POV character, then a verb, followed by a subject, similar to the example above (I promise I'll explain why later). On the next line (you can use the Tab key to get there) write a synopsis of the scene, whatever it is.

Pantsers, you are not forgotten. Let's say you just sit down and let monkeys fly from your backside, and those monkeys, prompted by the muse (and probably the thought of returning from whence they came at the end of their day), write your scene in all its first-draft glory. You can still use the synopsis function, by simply copying, say, the last paragraph of your scene into the synopsis. Again, there's a reason I suggest using the last paragraph which I promise will be revealed in the Organization section, later.

If, however, you just want to get some text into the synopsis card, there's an even easier way. On the Synopsis line, you'll see a little rectangle with a diagonal arrow. If you click it, the first paragraph or so of your text will magically appear in your synopsis window. Try it. We'll wait.

For now, let's move on to Preferences.

Preferences

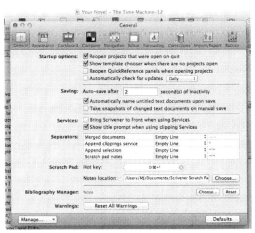

Figure 13: The General Preferences Window

Go ahead and click Scrivener > Preferences. You'll be presented with an incredibly extensive window that will allow you to adjust, tinker, and dink around with a bewildering number of aspects of the Scrivener

Interface. Some things you may want to change, others, you'll probably want to leave alone (if you take "probably" to mean "absolutely"). Change things slowly, and see what happens before you change too much and confuse yourself.

Notes:

SECTION 3

Digging deeper into Scrivener

Novel organization

In this section, we'll actually be doing stuff, like importing documents, naming chapters, setting Presets, compiling text, and saving your novel template.

Most of the things we've looked at are (with the exception of the Binder and the Inspector) functions you'd expect to find in an ordinary word processor. Now we get to the organization portion of Scrivener. This is where you get to lift your sword to the heavens and shout "By the power of Scrivener" and experience Scrivener's real potential.

**FYI—Do NOT actually walk into your yard, hold a sword up, and start shouting. The neighbors will not approve. Also, under NO circumstances, do so in the middle of a thunderstorm, because dude, *lightning*. At least the paramedics had a good laugh though.

We'll have to go back to the Binder for this exercise, so if you hid it (you did, didn't you, LOL), go ahead and make it visible.

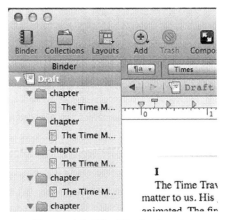

Figure 14: The Binder (again)

Okay, you're going to go up to the round, green Add button. Click and hold it. You'll see a popup window:

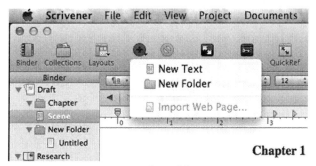

Figure 15: The Add Button

Click the folder icon. A new folder will appear in the Binder like magic. Now, before you go any further, go ahead and click the Add button again. You don't need to hold-click it this time. A new text file will appear under the folder. We're referring to the text file as a scene. You can have as many scenes in each chapter as you wish. Just add the next the same way, and the next, and so on.

Quick note: if you're paying close attention, you'll notice in Figure 15 above, the Scene icon is immediately below the uppermost Chapter icon, while the "Untitled" scene is moved to the right a bit under "New Folder." Good eye. This indicates the Scene isn't actually inside the chapter. Don't worry, this is easy to fix if it happens to you. Hold-click the Scene file and drag it until it sits right on top of the chapter folder. When you release the click, the Scene is now lined up properly, slightly to the right of the Chapter icon.

Text

Suppose you have a document you've already finished and would like to import it into Scrivener. There are three basic ways to accomplish this:

1. Copy/paste

This is pretty much what you're already used to if you use just about any word processor. You select the text you want to move and use the keyboard shortcut CMD + C (copy to clipboard) or CTRL + C if you're using a Windows computer. Move the cursor to where you want the text to show up and use the shortcut CMD + V (paste the text here). With computers running MS Windows, substitute CTRL (the control key) for CMD (the command key on a Mac).

2. Drag and Drop

Again, been there, done that, got the tee-shirt. Select the text to be copied, hold-click the mouse, and move the cursor to either the text's new home. Or, you could alternatively slide the cursor over to where you want your text to go in the Binder. Either way works equally well.

But there's a third option, also available in your favorite word processor, which you may not have used. Let's take a look.

3. Importing

Importing text is what it says. You click File > Import > and either Files or Import and Split. This last part is unique to Scrivener (and the other novel organizing software). A couple of cool things happen with Import; you don't need MS Word (or any other word processor, for that matter) on your computer to open a .doc or .docx or .odt formatted document. You just click the file you want and Scrivener will convert the text to .rtf for you and import it into your editor screen.

**A note here: Scrivener will import most common formats (.doc, .docx .rtf, and .odt), but it will convert them to .rtf, which is the worldwide standard text format (doing so also removes some, but not all the underlying extraneous formatting most word processors add to documents which causes most of the errors when uploading eBooks). More on that later.

When you import your text, you'll want to split the manuscript into scenes. One way is to place your cursor at the scene break and click Documents > Split and either at Selection or with Selection as Title.

If, when you wrote your manuscript, you used symbols at scene breaks, (a pound sign, three asterisks, etc.), you can tell Scrivener to split your manuscript at those symbols. Click File > Import > Import and Split. A pop-up window will appear. The lower half will have a sentence which says "Sections Are Separated By:" followed by a window where you can enter the symbol you used. Scrivener will split your manuscript into scenes at those symbols. Why is this a good idea? You'll find out when we get to Manipulating text in a minute. For now, try importing text all four ways. Don't worry, Scrivener won't mess with your original document.

Adding text

Let's say you'd like to add text to your work. That's easy. Just open up the Editor window, put your cursor what you want to start and let the monkeys fly.

Moving text

Now, you'd like to move text. If you're moving text within a scene (i.e. moving a paragraph to another position), you'll copy and paste, as you would've in your previous word processor. With one exception: instead of copying your selection to an invisible clipboard, you can store it temporarily in the Document Notes section of the Inspector. In this way, you'll know what you're moving, and you won't ever make the mistake of copying a section of text to the clipboard, and accidentally hitting copy again instead of paste, erasing your section of text. Let's see what it looks like in Figure 16:

Figure 16: Pasting into Documents (temporarily)

If, however, you'd like to shift a scene's position relative to the others, there's an easier way. Just single-click the scene in the Binder and drag it to the new position. Everything in that scene will change position automatically. That was pretty cool.

Many pantsers will be entirely satisfied with this level of functionality as will those writers who only compose shorter essays or short fiction stories. However, there are some very cool features to explore which will assist planners, hybrid writers, and even pantsers who would like additional control over the creative process. Let's go back to the Title Bar.

About word count

I know, I know, bigger isn't always better (that's my story and I'm sticking to it, anyway). But there comes a time in a writer's life when the conversation always turns to size, i.e. word count. What did you think I was talking about?

Anyway, those of you who aren't part of the degenerated masses often wonder what your novel has grown to in terms of word count. Most word processors will give a tally if asked,. Others will keep a running score, usually at the bottom of the window.

Scrivener does both.

And more.

The sharp-eyed amongst you may have noticed a word count in many of the illustrations so far. There's also a character count, I guess for the terminally obsessive-compulsive. There's another option, as well. Click Project > Show Project Targets, and you'll see a popup window that keeps a running count of your words as you type (Manuscript and Session Target). You can set the goals for either/both by clicking the zero after "of" and entering a number. If, say, your goal during NaNoWriMo is 1667 words per day, and your total goal is 50,000 words, you'd simply enter those numbers in the appropriate spots. Scrivener will not only keep track for you, a colored bar will grow across and change from red to green as you approach your goals.

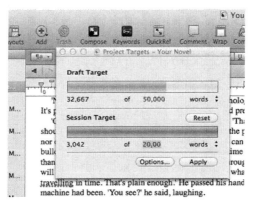

Figure 17: The Project Targets Window

If you click the "Options" button, you'll be presented with a window to set a monthly, weekly, and daily goals. That way, you'll know both how behind you're falling and the point at which you can finally give up and go for an ice cream cone. Oh, wait. That wasn't the point. Well, we can still get ice cream, right? I can catch back up. I only have to write 2500 words a day.

Anyway, if you click Projects > Project Statistics, you'll get a window which will compute how many printed and paperback pages your current work will need if/when printed. The final option, Text Statistics, will give you a count of words, paragraphs, lines, and even the frequency every word shows up in your work. It tracks everything, almost like the NSA designed the thing. Spooky.

Every November, it's like the thing is just sitting there, at the back of the barge, hammering out an increasingly rapid rhythm for the entire month. Then I find out it's only my heart speeding up as the weeks fly by.

Text Statistics is very handy if you want to know how many times you used the word "that," or "just," or "decapitate."

Notes:

Setting Presets

Bring in some short text (a few hundred words should be enough). We're going to set the formatting for the text body using the Format bar. When you're satisfied, select the appropriate text and click Format > Formatting > New Preset from Selection, and give it a snappy name, like Manuscript Body. I like my presets in all caps, so I know I made them. Looks something like Figure 18:

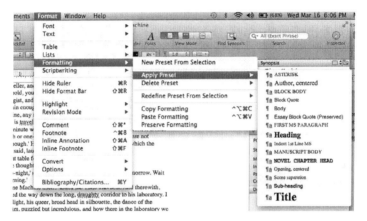

Figure 18: The Presets Menu

And you just do it for every element of your eBook, from Title and By Line, to Acknowledgments, for the entire manuscript and back matter.

Once your Presets are formatted, you can use them again and again for everything you write, because we're going to save this project as your personal novel template. If you need to add new Presets or change the existing, it's as easy as using "Redefine Preset From Selection."

You'll notice the process is a little different than setting/changing Styles in MS Word. In Scrivener, you'll set your desired formatting using the Format bar. Then, simply select the particular text and set the preset, rather than opening Styles and bringing up the formatting window. This is an example of how things used to be done when different minds approached problems differently, without trying to emulate MS Word.

If you change a Preset in your project, Scrivener will change the formatting of every instance where you used that preset, so you don't have to do it by hand. This becomes a huge deal if, say, you have a hundred and fifty chapters in a 200,000-word epic fantasy manuscript.

There's a really cool shortcut feature for applying presets in Scrivener, called the Presets Button. You'll find it directly below the Compose Button, see Fig. 19 below:

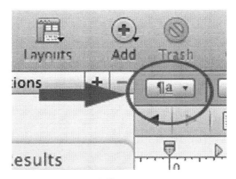

Figure 19: The Presets Button

Okay, what's next? Many people find they're more productive if they can get the distractions (like the ribbon, desktop background, etc. to disappear while they're writing. During the prehistoric ages of word processing, there was a blank screen, either blue or black, and your text composition, usually in white. If the programmer was fancy, the text was some obnoxious color (orange and green were popular). No distractions, no messing with formats, just composition.

There are programs that, when opened, cover your screen in a simple, bland color, and only show your text as you create it. Scrivener can do that as well with a feature called Full Screen Mode or Compose Mode. How does that work? We'll take a look in the next section.

Full Screen Mode

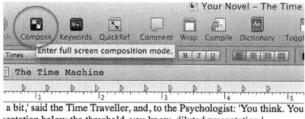

Figure 20: The Compose (Full Screen) Button

Composition Mode (Full Screen) can make most of your distractions go away (not all, though, your spouse, children, and pets are still yours to deal with).

So, if you click the little icon, what happens? This:

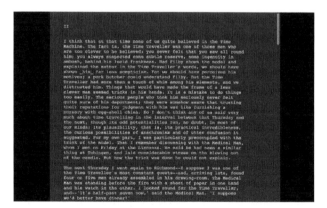

Figure 21: The Compose (Full Screen) Window

Okay, that looks good, but I'll bet you're wondering if there are there more ways to adjust the screen. Why yes, there are. Roll your mouse all the way to the bottom of the screen. You'll see something like Fig 22:

Figure 21: The Compose (Full Screen) Menu

Yes, You can change the font size to something easier to see, like:

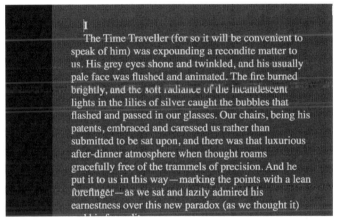

Figure 22: The Compose (Full Screen) Window

Tweak to your heart's content. You can change almost everything from the bar at the bottom or from Preferences, safe in the knowledge that none of it will make a bit of difference when you compile at the end. If you do copy-and-paste, as I sometimes do, you will have to fiddle with formatting. Those of you who use MS Word tell me it also has a full screen version now, but still doesn't do one important thing Scrivener does. Scrivener keeps the cursor vertically centered on the page. That means, as you type, instead of the cursor gradually drifting to the bottom of the screen and staying there, it stays mid screen. The text scrolls up, never leaving you with a cramped feeling like you're running out of space.

The Comment Button

Okay, you're writing along, and you're really cruising. The writing-monkeys have exited your butt en mass, and are screeching monkey-musings in your ear, and your fingers are an actual blur on the keyboard. You get to a point where you need to know some bit of trivia, like the muzzle velocity of a 9mm hollow point, or how long it'll take your character to asphyxiate if they get dumped out an airlock into space (isn't being a writer just the coolest thing?), but you don't want to stop, because *the monkeys*, dude.

In your old life, using MS Word :p or Open Office :p you would've had to resort to typing some lame gobbledygook like XXX or some such. Then you'd have to come back later when the monkeys were back in their corral and do a Find/Replace for all the XXXs and deal with them. But you are in your old life no longer. Now, what you'll do is select "muzzle velocity" or "9mm" in the text and click the little yellow sticky-note looking icon, and you'll get Figure 13:

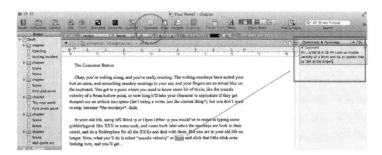

Figure 23: The Comment Button

So, you and the monkeys just keep on keeping on, until you or they tire, and you have time to go look things up.

Now, you just click on the yellow Comment (which takes you to the selected text in your manuscript), look the question up, address it, and click the X at the upper right of the Comment. It goes away, and you move on, secure in the knowledge that you won't miss any XXXs in your manuscript. Now wasn't that cool? If you get really good at it, you can pick four or five and look them all up, jot the information down, and take care of them by the bunch. This so beats "Find/Replace."

Oh, just so you know, Scrivener also has "Find/Replace," so you can find changes your editor sends you in an (ick) .doc formatted document. Type CMD+F to open it.

Ah, *cracks knuckles* enough MS Word bashing. Let's move on.

Setting up scenes

As in most things computer, there are at least two ways to open a new scene. The first way, for pantsers, is to open the first scene, start letting words fly, open a new scene as needed, and keep writing. You can do this easily in Scrivener. Add the next scene on the fly, either by using the Add button, left-clicking the binder and clicking Add > Text, or Add > New Text. Let's look at another way of doing the same thing.

If you'll look at the lower left corner, you'll see a plus sign and a folder icon/plus sign combination. Clicking the folder/+ sign will add a folder, and clicking the + sign will create a new text file.

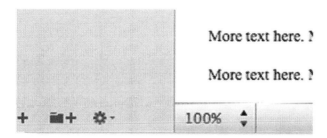

Figure 24: Alternative adding new scenes button

For you planners: You probably have a good idea how many words your book will be, and how many chapters it will need. If you like, you can simply add all those scenes up front.

I'm a planner. Maybe it's my engineering background, but I really like to have an idea how many rooms the building will have before I get to the job site. So here's what I do (your method and your madness will almost certainly be different). For convenience, we'll use mine this one time. Keep in mind, if you can come up with a way to organize your novel, Scrivener will almost certainly be able to accommodate your wishes.

Before we get started, let's understand each other. This isn't a how-to plot out you novel workbook. We're not saving any cats here, nor are we on a road trip with anybody named Joe Campbell. Whether you pitch tent pole moments or just pants the crap out of your novel, or whatever, is fine. All we're doing is setting up some kind of a template you're comfortable with and you'll want to use to write your novel. Heck, you can change it, dink around with it, delete it, or go sit in the hot tub. Are we good, then? Okay. Let's crank this thing up and get rolling.

We're going to make some huge assumptions for a moment. Let's assume your book will have 80,000 words (more or less). For the sake of argument, let's also assume your book will consist of four acts: Act 1, Act 2, Act 3, and Act 4 (Acts 2&3 make up the traditional Act 2 - thanks, Larry Brooks for putting that in my head). This works out to 20,000 words +/- in each act (I also like round numbers). Let's further assume, the total book will have either twenty-four or thirty-two chapters when we're done ('cause - math). That works out to six-eight chapters per act, each chapter being composed of (roughly) 2500-3333 words, or ten-fourteen printed pages. Again, this only gives us some goals. So, we're going to make four folders and add the correct number of files, knowing we can always add or subtract later. That looks something like Figure 25:

Figure 25:

Another way might be to create a new folder for each chapter, like this:

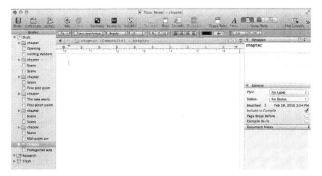

Figure 26:

Yet another way might be to disregard the folders completely and only create text file scenes, naming them as you go. It's your template, build it however you wish. Scrivener can handle it, trust me.

So, here's what I do (again it's just one way); I create twenty-four folders, name them according to the plot points I'm writing toward, and create a text file in each (because a chapter can't have less than one scene, no matter how lean your writing is). I can name those files for what plot milestones I'm shooting for (Opening, Inciting incident, First plot point, Statement of stakes, etc.). If you decide (as I often do) the keep your scenes to 1300-1800 words, I just create more text files, as needed.

You'll notice all the folders in the figures have a little gray triangle immediately to the left of the icon. That triangle means something is in the folder (your chapters/scenes). Clicking the triangle hides or makes the text visible. Try it. We'll wait.

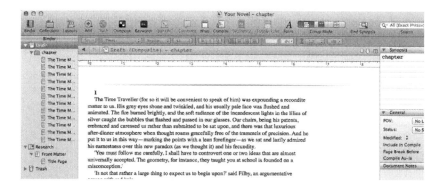

Figure 27:

Notes:

MICHAEL J. CARLSON

Naming scenes

You probably went ahead and named all your text files "Scene 1, Scene 2, Scene 3, etc." What? You went ahead and named all your text files…Scene 1, Scene 2, etc? What were you thinking? Don't you know the fabric of the universe is in danger? Dude…

That's fine, as long as all your scenes are in exactly the right position. But what do you do if you decide Scene 16 works better right after Scene 9? In a word processor (I'll refrain from mentioning any names here), you would highlight the scene you want to move, copy the text to the invisible clipboard, delete it from where it was, and insert it into its new position. Unless you accidentally put it in behind Scene 8 instead of Scene 9, in which case imaginative expletives ensue.

But this is Scrivener, not some overpriced, bloated word processor designed by a bunch of marketing monkeys. Since you created all your text files in the appropriate places (you did, didn't you?), you'll simply drag that pesky text from Scene 16 into the Binder behind Scene 9. Guess what—all the text went as a unit. And if you change your mind or find a place the text works better—just drag it to its new position. If you change your mind and want the scene back in its original position, there's a do-over. Remember those keyboard shortcuts? It's time for one. If you decide to undo the most recent thing you did, press the CMD+Z (CTRL+Z on a Microsoft machine). Scrivener will undo the last thing you did, whatever it was.

Oh, one thing you'll notice anyway, so I'll tell you ahead of time; you can't move scenes between folders in corkboard view. This is okay if you used folders for acts, but not so much if you made a bunch of folder-chapters, 'cause now you can't move the scenes. Except you can. You just have to move scenes between folders in the outliner view. Don't worry, Scrivener will let you.

Which brings us to a better way to name your scenes. If you decided your story was better served by having the old Scene 16 after Scene 9, you would be forced to renumber everything according to the new order. This might be significant if you have a lot of scenes. Some authors I know write novels of over a hundred chapters. If you make additional changes, the chance for errors multiply.

Another possibility to consider is what happens with small changes? For instance, you need to make Princess Leia's ship larger or smaller, but gosh, you can't remember in which three scenes it's mentioned. Uh-oh.

How about if, instead of naming scenes numerically, we name them according to what happens in them? We could do that with scenes, as well, because as people, we typically remember stories better than chapter numbers and those details will help us remember where the information was. So, now, we can find the three spots in the story where the Princess' ship is described. Since they'll be much easier to find (and we can ignore the six other places where the ship is only mentioned).

In my experience, naming scenes by what happens at the end is more efficient. Writing toward the end of the scene gives me a goal and keeps me moving forward, but you can name your scenes any way you wish.

Also, it's important to keep in mind that naming the scenes at this stage has no bearing on what's compiled at the end. The names we use at the composition stage aren't necessarily included. We can let Scrivener add Chapter 1, 2, 3, etc. automatically when it compiles, or we can make the changes manually. Remember, Scrivener works for us, not the other way around.

An example

Let's set up an example to illustrate. I've downloaded a copy of The Time Machine by H.G. Wells from the Gutenberg Project website. I saved the text as an .rtf file and copied the first three chapters into Scrivener and split them into chapters (I, II, and III). Let's see what it looks like.

Figure 28:

If you'll look at the Binder in Figure 28, you'll see the first chapter of Act 1 is selected. The text showing in the Editor is the text located in that chapter. I've named it "The Traveler Proposes Time Travel." Immediately to the right of the Editor window, in uppermost rectangle, you'll find the same title with a short synopsis of how the chapter ends. If we were writing this chapter, the synopsis would be what we're writing toward as a goal. In the gray area just below the Synopsis, there's no POV or Status information because I haven't added any, yet. Sharp-eyed reader you are, though, you'll notice I did change Label (the default) to POV. This is easily done by clicking the "No Label" pop-up and choosing "edit" at the bottom. There's also a Roman numeral "I" at the very top of the text in the editor. If we tell Scrivener not to add chapter titles automatically (which it can do), this would become the chapter title.

**A word about POV instead of Label
In a little while, we'll discuss why this might be a good idea. Go ahead and change Label to POV now. You can always change it back or to something else later if you decide it doesn't work for you.

The next scene, or Chapter II, is titled "The Traveler returns." The synopsis is also different from Chapter I. We'll get into the significance of the Synopsis area of the Inspector now.

Planning

Planning a novel is relatively easy in Scrivener. Let's look at two functions, the Corkboard, and the Outliner.

Corkboard Mode

One of Scrivener's more powerful functions, especially for planners, is the corkboard mode. A good way to think of Corkboard Mode is having the synopsis of every scene in your novel pinned to a corkboard on your wall. This is similar to the storyboarding process done for movies, except we're using words instead of pictures. If you recall, we mentioned switching Mode back when we discussed the Title Bar. It looks like this:

Figure 29: Edit Scrivenings Button

Select Manuscript at the top of the binder, then open the corkboard by clicking the center icon in View Mode. You should see something like this:

Figure 30: The Corkboard Button

Which changes your editor screen to:

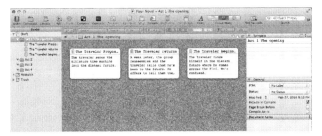

Figure 31: The Corkboard View (named so for obvious reasons)

Single-click the first index card. If the Inspector is open, you'll notice the titles of the two match. Any text you enter into one will be reflected in the other automatically. Try it.

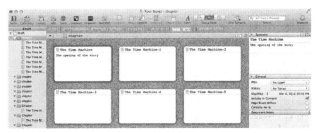

Figure 32: Index Cards and Sybopsis Window contain the same info

This is the place where you'll write the synopsis of each chapter.

NOTICE

If you chose to create a folder for each chapter and put files in each, you'll notice there appear to be multiple cards under each folder on the corkboard. That's because if we set the structure to include chapter folders containing files from the start, we can only view chapters on the corkboard from the Draft level. Corkboard only shows one level at a time—in this case, it's the chapter level. If we move to an individual chapter folder, we'll see all the scenes within that chapter. If we click each scene, by holding down the CMD (CTRL on Windows) key and clicking the scenes, we'll see them in order but we can't change the order. The only way we can move scenes is within the chapter where they're contained. Now, you understand why I didn't recommend that process off the bat, right? Using act folders is pretty safe. You're unlikely to decide to move a scene from Act 3 into the opening, but you may want to rearrange scenes within an act. Again, your template, your rules. Either way works.

Okay, let's pretend you listened to my advice and lined your chapters (or scenes, if you prefer) as text files within the act folders. It'll look something like in Figure 33:

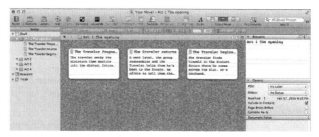

Figure 33: Binder/Corkboard/Synopsis

If you decide later a particular scene works better in a different location, you'll be able to reposition it easily by drag and drop on the corkboard. You'll know what's in the scene by its title/synopsis and the titles and synopses of the scenes in front of and behind the new position. Try it.

But, let's say you're visually oriented, as I am. Maybe you'd like to load something visual into your index card for when you storyboard. Scrivener can do that. Just do the old drag and drop. It'll look something like Figure 34:

Figure 34: Drag a picture into the Synopsis Window...

Now, we can see what that would look like. Click the Act 1 folder and switch to Corkboard view. Yours should look like this:

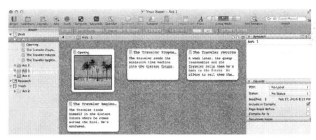

Figure 35: ...and it also shows up in the Index Card

And when you're editing, if you decide you want that scene at Ft. Lauderdale Beach after chapter III, just hold-click and drag it to the correct position.

Figure 36: Repositioning an Index Card

The astute reader will notice the position of The Opening has also changed to after "The Traveler Begins," or the forth position in Act 1. Scrivener does this automatically with any file you move on the

Corkboard. Try it a few times. Anything you do to an Index Card in Corkboard view, happens automatically to its corresponding synopsis window and vice-versa. Let's look at the Outliner mode next.

Outliner Mode

The Outliner (AKA Group Mode) is the icon on the far right of View Mode. Click it.

Figure 37: The outliner button

and you'll see:

Figure 38: The outliner window

The Outliner Mode (Group Mode) is similar to but different from the Corkboard. It might help to think of it as a spreadsheet for your novel. You can move your chapters, scenes, and even your acts around in this window, you can also add metadata to your chapters, scenes, and acts. Why is this important? Well, as an example, remember when I changed "Label" to "POV?" we're about to find out why. Let's say you named your scenes with the "POV character, verb, subject" example from earlier. You could enter the POV character in the appropriate space and even color code the scene/chapter line according to the character., Doing so would make it clear at a glance how long since a particular character had a chapter. This is only one way to set up the Outliner. If you want to see what it can really do, click the little double arrow in the upper right corner which looks like this: >>

You'll see:

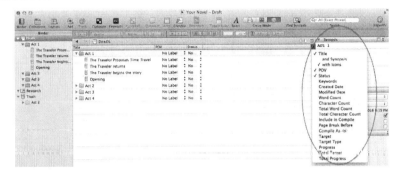

Figure 39: Working with the outliner

Or, alternatively, go up to the View button and click it.

Figure 40:

You can fiddle with these to your heart's content, knowing if you want to change something in the future, you can.

Notes:

SECTION 4

Setting the Compile function

If you recall, we mentioned early on that unless you copy/paste your work to get it out of Scrivener, the text formatting settings in your Editor screen are meaningless to your book's final formatting. This is because, unlike a word processor, what you see in Scrivener is separate from what you get as output.

Remember way back in Let's Get Started, when we said Scrivener re-separates composition from typesetting? This is where the typesetting part happens. Think of this part of the software as a built-in desktop publisher. There are a few things Scrivener is unable to do, like drop caps and changing lead size, but you'll be able to format your manuscript to make distribution easier. Setting the Compile function gives you the most control over your finished product, and can be therefore somewhat overwhelming. We'll go slowly. Keep in mind this is a superficial overview of what Compile is capable of. And remember, if you make a mistake, you can always go back and reset whatever is giving you wonky output.

This output control is called the Compile function, and you can set or reset it at any time from File > Compile. The window looks like this:

Figure 41: Compile window

In Compile function, you'll be able to choose the font and size of your text, page formatting, which text is included, print settings, metadata, scene and chapter separators, and more.

You'll be able to format for: eBook (with or without parts, iBooks Author Chapters, Nonfiction Manuscript, Paperback Novel (with or without Parts), Plain Text Screenplay (Movie Magic), Script or Screenplay, Standard Manuscript, Synopsis and Titles, Synopsis Outline, or Custom.

You'll also be able to set print for: Rich Text (.rtf), Plain Text (.txt), Microsoft Word (.doc or .docx), Open Office (.odt), pdf, ePub (.epub), Kindle Book (.mobi), Final draft 5-7 (.fcf), Final Draft 8 (.fdx), and PDF (.pdf).

Compile is a new concept for most people and a fairly complex option, so we'll go slowly.

Notes:

Specifying Compile settings

When setting your own Compile options, it's always good to start with Original (not extra crispy). Okay, bad joke, sorry. Original is the option you want in Format As. You could start with one of the standard formats options, but if you start with Original and create your own you'll be more comfortable changing things later.

Original simply compiles your document as is, putting a blank space between each document. First, we need to move from Compile Summary to All Options. In the Compile window, you'll notice the first option in the left-hand column is Contents.

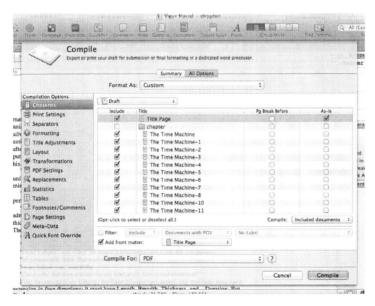

Figure 42: Contents

Here's where we can check and uncheck various boxes to include or exclude any text file or folder we like. We can also force a page break before any text file or folder. This usually isn't necessary, as it's normally set in Separators, but it's nice to know you could do it here if you wanted to for one specific document or folder. The column on the far right contains a column of boxes labeled As-Is. Check these boxes to compile with your text exactly as it is currently in your editor, based on how you set up your Presets to begin with. If you do this, though, and you wrote your manuscript in Helvetica 16 point, that's how the finished product will compile, ensuring a stream of colorful expletives from your editor. Ignore any other settings in contents. Hopefully, you won't need to mess around with these. You'll notice the third item down in the left-hand column is Separators. If you click it now, you'll see something like Figure 43:

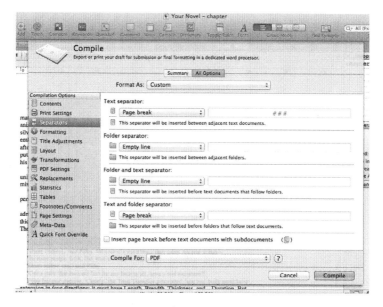

Figure 43: Separators

Notice Text separator, Folder separator, and Folder and text separator are set to have an empty line between documents. Text and Folder Separator has a page break specified. If you were to compile now, you would see exactly this in your text, including the page break after the end of text in each chapter.

Now we'll move on to formatting.

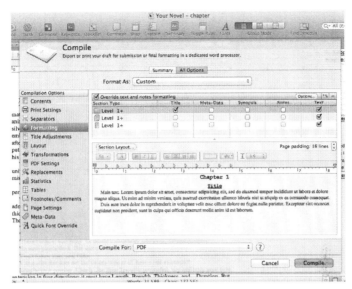

Figure 44: Formatting

Here, we have different types of documents (Folders, Text level containers, and Text files) in the window on the right. Initially, all 3 are sent to include text (those boxes are checked). You'll notice the Folders contain no text, so in this case whether at the box is checked or not makes no difference. If, however, you wrote a Folder-level synopsis, you'd want to uncheck this box, so as not to include the synopsis in your finished product. Most of the time, fiction manuscripts will have no text containers (text files which have other text files nested under them). So whether the box is checked are not typically makes no difference, either. However, we may as well uncheck those boxes just to be safe in the future. You can always re-check them later if you need to.

You'll also notice the box next to "Override text and notes formatting" at the top of the window is also unchecked. That tells us our current presets (remember that Helvetica 16 point you loved so much when you were writing?) will be used when compiling. Expect a nasty email from your editor.

Click on Transformations next.

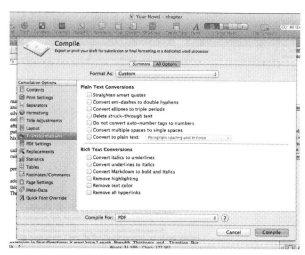

Figure 45: Transformations

This is for old-timers who insist on writing in Courier New font, underlines instead of italics, straight quotes, two spaces between sentences, etc., like when people used typewriters. You can switch between double hyphens and em dashes and all the stuff that nice Vonda McIntyre lady recommends as "Typesetting Marks." Do NOT set up your Compile functions to do all that stuff if you're uploading to an eBook distributor (i.e. Amazon, Kobo, or Smashwords). The people who buy your masterpiece will not like you. Remember, YOU are the typesetter now, not some gnarled old geezer in a leather apron. In fact, it's probably best to uncheck all of them, so you don't upload it that way inadvertently. The problem happens when your reader changes the text size in their eReader and your three-period ellipsis or double-hyphen em dash gets split onto the next line or worse, the next page. If you're one of those old-timers who, like me, learned on a typewriter, and you can't stand to see your text formatted in anything but Courier New, no offense meant. Just remember to set the transformations to get rid of that stuff. Could be worse, at least it's not Helvetica 16 point.

The only other compilation option to worry about for now is page settings, toward the bottom of the window. Click that now.

This is what you should see:

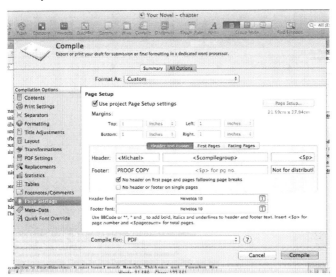

Figure 46: Page settings

You'll see it's set up by default to use your project title as the default header. Take a look at Header and Footer. You'll notice a string of gibberish there. Those are called Special Tags, and they tell Scrivener to go gather specific information from your project and put it in the specified places. For instance, right now your project is set up to automatically put your project's name and page numbers in the header and footer, respectively. Pretty neat, don't you think?

**Please note: Special tags can be found under Help > Placeholder tags. You enter information in these special tags by going to Project > Meta-Data Settings > Project Properties and entering the information in the appropriate space.

The Compile settings are the reason your document output will appear the way you want it to, no matter what you did to it in the editor (with caveat, which we'll talk about in a moment).

Now, *laughs maniacally* let's start changing these settings.

Go back to the Binder. Create a text file entitled "Title Page" anywhere you like and drag it to directly under "Draft" just above the first folder.

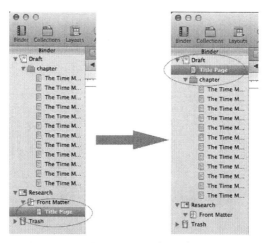

Figure 47: Moving the title page

Rather than creating our own title page, we'll copy/paste all the information from the Standard Novel Template in Scrivener. Open the template, select all on the Title Page, and copy it to your Title Page now. If you choose the Paperback Title Page, it will look like this:

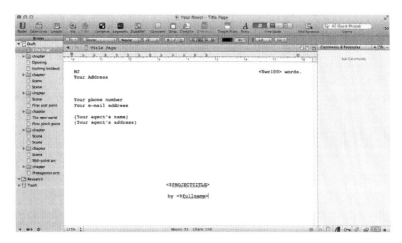

Figure 48: Paperback title page

Yeah, the font is a little big. You can change the title to about 18 points, and the by-line to about 14 points. That's good for most eBooks. The ebook format doesn't come with a Title Page, but I like to include one in mine, and I use the Paperback Page.

There's another page available, called Manuscript. Let's look at it.

Figure 49: Manuscript title page

There are quite a few more Project Tags on this page than the previous one. This would be more consistent with what you'd use to submit to an agent. If you go to Format > Options > Show Invisibles, you'll see this page is set up the tables included. Go ahead and hide the invisibles again.

If we compiled at this point, because there's a folder after the text document, it would have a page break, which is as it should be. But (and that's a big but), if you compile now, you'd also notice a header and footer on the title page. This is considered, um, let's say not the most professional way to deliver a manuscript. So, we'll correct that next.

Reopen the Compile window again. We can remove the header and footer one of two ways. Either check "No header on first page and pages following page breaks." The second way is to click "First Pages" and check "Different first pages header and footer." Either works.

If you look closely, you'll see "Page numbers count first pages" is also checked. If we left this alone, the page number would be absent from the first page, but the second page would start with page two. Again, not what we would prefer, so just uncheck the box.

This is a good time to stop for a second and save what you've done so far. Hold down the option key and click Compile to save your settings so far.

Notes:

Finishing up specifying Compile settings

If you recall, we had the front page at the top, right before our first chapter. We can also create another folder called "Front Matter" outside the Draft (in Research, for instance). Move the Title page to the new folder, go back to Contents, and check the "Add Front Matter" option at the bottom of the window, right here, in Figure 50:

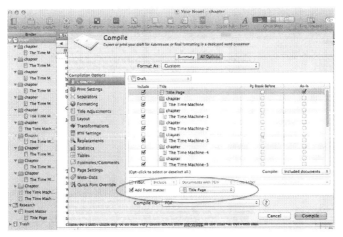

Figure 50: Add front matter

Totally cosmetic change: Your front matter folder can have a special icon. Right click the Front Matter folder and click "Front matter." Note: you can change icons while you're writing your book to signify first draft, second draft, etc., including editing and finished. Scrivener is very generous with icons. Change them simply by right-clicking in the Binder.

Just for the sake of argument, let's say you want to replace the empty space between your novel's scenes with a symbol. Go back to Compile, Separators, and replace "Empty Space" with "Custom." The default is a pound symbol, but if you go to Edit > Special Characters, you'll see a popup window with oodles of specialized symbols. You can use any you like by clicking the one you want.

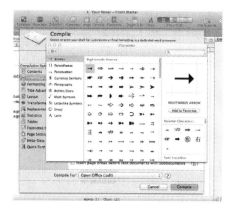

Figure 51: Special symbols

Next, we'll want to add chapter numbering. In Formatting, select the folder (level 1+) and click Section Layout. In the popup window, you'll type "Chapter" followed by a special tag for auto numbering. You'll add that by Edit > Insert > Auto-number and choose the one you want.

Figure 52: Chapter numbering

Add a carriage return (the enter key) after the special tag for numbering so there's a space between your chapter number and chapter title.

Did I just say chapter title?

Yes. What if you want an actual Chapter Title for your chapters?

Chapter titles

Okay, what if you're one of the people for whom a simple Chapter _(number)_ isn't enough, and you like chapter titles with your eggs and your beer? Scrivener can do that for you. Just go back to Compile, Formatting:

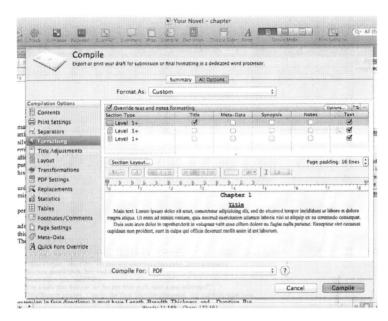

Figure 53: Chapter naming

You can change any of the text formatting in the text window at the bottom. Remember, this is for output only, and won't affect what you see when you write your next book. It'll still be in (gag) Helvetica 16 point font. You can change the font to Courier if your agent requests it. Or you can change the output font to Times New Roman or Georgia or whatever you'd like your eBook text to be (being cautious not to get too esoteric). Some eReaders may not have the bizarre font your mom likes, and your text will default to the closest approximation (like Times New Roman) or give an error message.

What if you want to get artsy and start your chapters about halfway down the page? You won't want to do this for an eBook. It'll muck up the text flow if your reader changes font size too much and you don't want your reader to be unhappy. But, in case your mom's really pushing for the text in her printed copy to start lower on the page, change the page padding to 10-12 lines in the Formatting window.

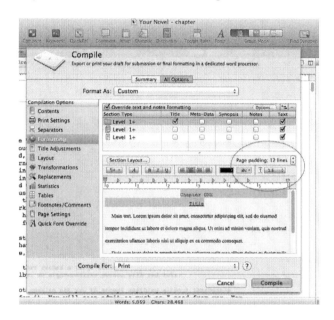

Figure 54: Starting the chapter down the page

Okay, Mom, happy?

If you want your paragraphs to all have the same first-line indent, this window is also where you'll set this up. There's a ruler at the top of the text window. Right above the ruler, you'll notice little blue triangles. On the far left, above the "0", you should see a downward facing triangle and a little blue rectangle above it. That rectangle controls the first-line indent, so you'll move it to the position you want all your manuscript first lines set to. Suppose you change your mind and want the first lines of each scene to be flush left. Up above, you'll find an "Options" button to the right of "Override text and formatting." Clicking that button opens another window, as in Figure 55:

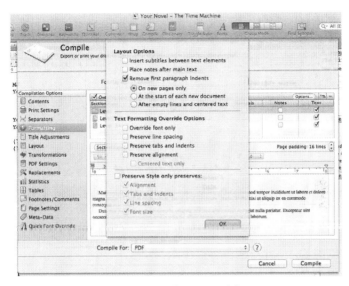

Figure 55: Override text and formatting

Click the "After empty lines and centered text" button and click OK.

Saving your template

Hopefully, we've stayed together so far. If you followed along, you should have most of the settings for your novel template in the ballpark. And you should have a good idea how to tweak them when you need/want to.

To recap: The important things you did. You set your Binder to contain four Act folders, each with 6-8 text files, named for the usual parts of a novel (or one of the other alternatives). You've set your Editor screen to your preferred text font and size for writing in either the Preferences window or using Presets, knowing the output will be handled by the Compile function. Then you set your preferred settings in the Outliner and you set the Corkboard to show the Index Cards the way you prefer (both layout and color). And you've created and set the formatting for your Presets so you can control your text formatting as you go.

Finally, you deleted all the imported text, anything you added to the Research section you don't need, and emptied the Trash.

All that's left is to save your template. Click Format As > Manage Compile Presets and click the "+" sign in the lower left. You'll see something closely resembling Figure 56:

Figure 56: Manage compile presets

Type in the name of your novel template and click OK.

Congratulations. You've set up your own novel template in Scrivener. It will be available for your use throughout your career, which I hope is long and enjoyable.

Notes:

Final thoughts

I would like to take a moment to thank Keith Blount for all the work he did, developing a piece of software that actually works. His was a monumental effort, and he deserves the undying gratitude of novelists everywhere.

Again, this workbook is my own creation, and is in no way affiliated with Mr. Blount, Scrivener, or Literature and Latte. Nor is it meant to take the place of The Scrivener Manual or The Interactive Tutorial, but should be used in conjunction with those fine documents. This workbook discusses certain aspects of the Scrivener software that adapters may have difficulty with. Readers are encouraged to refer to The Scrivener Manual, The Interactive Tutorial, and several You Tube videos offered by Literature and Latte, the makers of Scrivener.

I hope you found the exercises in this workbook helpful. If you enjoyed it, or if you have any helpful suggestions on improving the contents, please drop me a note at: michael@mjcarlson.com.

Okay, you're at the end. Go, play. Do good work. Remember, life is hard, wear a helmet.

Oh, and one more thing:

"This work was produced without using any Microsoft products."

THE END

Notes:

Notes:

Made in the USA
Middletown, DE
30 December 2017